THE MICROGOLF PRIMER:

RAISE GOLF ACRES IN YARDS

BY
BRIAN L. MCGONEGAL

WITH
DAVID C. ENGER

MICROGOLF ≤≥ PRESS

JACKSON, MICHIGAN

1997

Copyright © 1997 by Microgolf ≤≥ Press

All rights reserved
including the right of reproduction
in whole or in part in any form.

Printed on acid-free paper.

Cover and binding materials have been chosen
for strength and durability.

Manufactured in the United States of America

First Edition

2 4 6 8 10 12 11 9 7 5 3 1

ISBN 0-9658430-0-9

Table of Contents

FOREWORD
Golf and Microgolf 2

CHAPTER 1
Journey a Round with me 4

CHAPTER 2
Tools and Equipment 15
Introduction 15
Mower, Reel Type 17
Cup Cutter 17
Garden Rake 18
Broom Rake 18
Thatching Rake 18
Pitchfork 19
Dinner Fork 20
Aerating Tool 20
Cups 20 • Pins 21
Tee Numerals & Markers 21
Cup Puller 22
Grass Seed 23
Conclusion 24

TABLE OF CONTENTS

CHAPTER 3
Course Layout and Development 25
Tees 25
Distances 29
Plantings 30
Borders and Boundaries 31

CHAPTER 4
Green Development 33
Slope 33
Undulation 34
Shape 35
Height of Grass 38
Birth of the Green 39
Nursery 46
Apron 47
Sand Traps 48
Cup Cutting 51
Cup Placement 53

Table of Contents

CHAPTER 5
Time Line 55

CHAPTER 6
Green Maintenance 58
Cutting the Green 58
Fertilizing 59
Sanding or Top Dressing 60
Aerating 62
Moving the Cup 63
Also used for Damage Control
Transplanting Technique
Divots, and Marks on the Green 64
The Dent 66
The Split Dent 67
Flap or Dislodged Divot 67
Cleat Marks 69
Problems & Preventions 70
Weeds 70
Fungus & Mold 71
Worms & Grubs 72
Neighbors 73

TABLE OF CONTENTS

CHAPTER 7
Playing by Microgolf Rules 76
Definition of Microgolf 76
Putts 77
Par 77
Order of Play 78
Ball Marking 79
Pins 80
Out of Bounds 80
Unplayable Lie 81
Clubs 82

AFTERWORD
The Dream Links Legend 84

THE MICROGOLF PRIMER:

RAISE GOLF ACRES IN YARDS

FOREWORD
Golf and Microgolf

I HAVE KNOWN people who had putting greens.

I say "had" because just putting is rather boring, and the greens return to "from whence they came."

Harvey Penick knew that putting practice should be chipping onto the green, then putt out.

No gimmes.

He also stated, for a warmup limited by time, that you are better off doing the same chipping and putting routine.

I found, by cutting a green and designating tee boxes, the same exhilarating thrill of first tee jitters and pride of making a good clean shot onto the green.

Fifty feet or five hundred yards make no difference: the challenge is the same, the reward just as satisfying when the ball finds the bottom of the cup. This game *is* golf — except in a micro course layout.

Golf and Microgolf · 3

Variations of the game bear little resemblance to golf and all its pleasures.

Microgolf has *all* of those pleasures in a fraction of the time. I have played eighteen holes in twenty minutes, a foursome in one hour. I even host an annual thirty-six-hole tournament in one afternoon. Friends have built their own courses and started tournaments. We are now making our own Microgolf tour.

The most misunderstood portion of the golf course is the making of the green. Several people told me: "You can't make your own green, it's too expensive to do and you'll spend too much time on maintenance."

My thoughts were; Cut the grass short, buy the cups, and start playing.

Although it sounds slightly naïve, if you have healthy grass growing now that *is* about all there is to it.

There are some things you'll need to know and some things you'll need to buy.

So with this knowledge you too can have a Microgolf course.

1 Journey a Round with me

Can you tell how the Dream Links play from looking at the cover? Of course the order is clear: one through eighteen for tees and a separate green for the first and second nines.

I wish the cover map were holographic 3-D or at least a pop-up to help you see what I do when I step up to each tee; the green's slope difference from one tee to the next; selecting a shot to land on a spot and roll correctly over undulation and into the cup. A stand of lilacs that are not directly in the ball flight-path but can be in my peripheral vision enough to shift my focus and attention and lead to a missed green.

George Perrot, a pioneer travellogue television host from the early days took one to the far corners of the world with weekly guests.

Journey a Round with me · 5

Please be my guest and journey with me to the corners of the Dream Links. Find each tee on the cover as you read the hole's description.

Hole number one, a simple 22.0-foot tee shot, induces jitters as real as any first tee. The slope of the green is north to south, with a slope change toward the first tee box and cup in the center of the green. I play a sand wedge hooded, the ball way back in my stance, add a strong putt-style stroke, no wrist action, land the ball slightly left of the straight line to the cup so the ball rolls up the slope and breaks to my right when it encounters the slope break from north to south. An eagle, a hole in one, for they are all par 3s, if the ball goes in, or a simple birdie with one putt. That's unless I shank, blade, stroke too hard, or misalign. It is the first hole after all, and maybe I underestimate the hole or overestimate my focus of attention initially.

Hole two, different for the distance, 19.5 feet, and the break between slopes creates a ridge west to east, the direction I'm facing. I align just left of the pin and hit the ball in the middle of my stance, putt-like, no wrist, a little spin and the ball rolls on the ridge until some left to right slope pushes the ball to the south side of the ridge and breaks to the cup. Too much spin and the ball hangs on the apron slope. Hit too hard and it may be in the trap, too soft and the ridge takes over and I'm in the yucca nested in the hollow of the kidney-bean- shaped green.

The third's approach direction accents the slope and requires a little wrist and spin to stay on the green. It's 21.0 feet.

The fourth demands a lot of wrist harder hit. Don't let the topiary bush, cut to look like a cat, break your concentration at your left. The tendency on the 23.0-foot hole is to leave the ball short. For fear of its rolling off the other side. Hello, yucca; and pressure's on to produce par.

Journey a Round with me · 7

The fifth misses the trap but the box is five feet above the green and reverses the slope right to left, travels over a two-foot dip before the green, rolls the balance of the 33.0 feet and can catch the first tee's green slope and off toward the twelfth tee box.

Number six, three feet above the green and a four-foot bush right in front of you off the tee demands a high cut, land short and roll toward the cup if it hasn't rained recently leaving the ground soft and the ball to remain short. The slope runs directly away from you and you can't see the cup for the bush.

The pin on seven peeks just over the sight line from the tee box over a downward spiral-cut bush that totals eight feet from top to bottom on the green side and sand trap in between making the landing area on the north side of the trap. 38.0 feet in total.

The view from eight is 40.0 feet, the first nine's longest hole, diagonal between lilacs on the left and seven's spiral bush a five foot drop to the cup. Land the ball at the southwest corner of the trap yet miss it.

The trap is in play for the 24.5 foot five-foot elevation on nine as you see the bottom of the cup conspires with the landing area to spit the ball back into the sand.

All except numbers one and two will be off the green if you land it on. The turn back toward the clubhouse requires a deep sigh of relief as you know that as difficult as the progression of holes you have encountered that, without a doubt, the number one handicap hole is number ten.

Ten: the longest hole at 50.0 feet is also the shortest landing area making the drop box the usual second shot and third stroke. If not for the drop box, perhaps the round would never end as O.B. is loss of distance as well as a stroke penalty. Players can always hit the tee ball towards the number five tee up the five-foot slope of rough that may hold the ball from going O.B. This option with the cup in the center of the green still confronts you with a long putt from the rough up a two-foot slope in the green to the cup, otherwise beyond the cup the crown of the green rolls the ball O.B. at the south and back off to the drop box for your fourth stroke. Bogey is just fine.

Rather than the safe shot, wimping out, eleven is over the spiral cut bush and difficult to stick. Aim is directed towards number eight tee box as the longest landing dimension, 42.5 feet to the center and a longer than rough cut. Your margin of error.

The second nine's crowned green, some crown south but mostly north, peaks just south of center three feet at the summit to the north tip of the pear shape means the twelfth's 40.0-foot tee shot is a safer shot than ten, but may catch the crown, roll down the north direction and definitely into the rough. Par may still be possible. The safe route is not an option as the tee's south placement creates a diagonal directly into the bushes between five and six. No safety- valve, wimp-out tee shot on this hole!

Thirteen is a 38.0-foot option up the safety valve slope, but the long diagonal of the green's area presents a very makeable shot if you practice as if you were going to play Carnegie Hall. Ten through thirteen is my Amen Corner but after that, the devil still lurks. Keep your focus.

Fourteen's 26.5 feet — we endearingly call it "the yucca" — can be a "no-brainer" or a futile attempt at clearing the wall or another visit to the drop area, and "they" want to call it a putt.

Even though fifteen's 24.0 feet are level until the green rises as one large undulation, it does fall one and a half feet after the crest to O.B. and back to the drop box, or if you land on the slope with backspin, the ball will roll down the hill that is the safety valve alley approach for number eleven tee shot in the vicinity between the sand trap and the sixteenth tee. Bogey if you're lucky.

With that experience it seems as though sixteen's 26.0 feet would be a reliable par; however, the spiral bush blocks vision of, and approach line of a large portion of the green, and includes an additional rearward slope towards number eight tee after clearing a six foot elevation and a portion of that bush. Makeable but a sleeper, the ball might decide to roll back to your feet. More practice? The hole may set up for lefties as the spiral bush is on the right side of the approach alleyway. However, southpaws don't necessarily agree.

"The wall" four feet high is the nickname for seventeen's 17.0 feet, a coincidence not lost on me, easy if you can get the ball up as high as fast as you can as your club head feels like it's going to clip the concrete retaining wall. Or are we getting real good from the drop box tee?

Eighteen and we're 30.5 feet from home, already? Aw, shucks! The same hazards as fifteen but longer. You have to hit it harder but the landing area is shorter by comparison. Hit into the green's exaggerated slope at the pear tip and potentially more practice from down around the sixteenth tee box, and I always want to end up with a birdie. If only desire kept my score.

Handshakes and high five's around. The disclosure of scores reaffirming our habit of declaring after every hole—the hole score and our individual overall score if there was a change. Parring is the exception from repeating the overall score.

Eighteen holes complete, this replay travelogue is idealized for the number and kinds of shots, for the places I might end up in are limitless. Every hole has been made in one. All holes have been the ruination of a record round. As soon as I think any hole is a guaranteed birdie, I can bogey it. The ball's position after my tee shot determines, miss the green in the sand trap and a sand save is required for a par. If my first putt is too strong, then I may end up three putting and a bogey. But a hole in one, an eagle, birdie, bogey or dreaded other are all possible. Gee, this sounds like a round of golf, in an hour? No apologies, no gimmes, no kidding.

Thank you for joining me on this Dream Links journey. As I recall, the record round of thirteen under was a six then seven under. I was better on the more difficult second nine. That utterly astounds me. In fact, I limit beginners to the safer first nine until their fundamentals will allow them to finish.

How can you join me for the next tee time? The first step you took by starting *The Microgolf Primer*. I already know you appreciate the nature of golf by this start. There are still shadows of doubt in your mind. First and foremost, there's the expense of tools and equipment and just where have you got room to store all that stuff. Relax and read on. I reveal all and more. The secret is in the fun, not work; efficiency, not time. After all, I'm in a hurry to go play another eighteen holes.

2 Tools and Equipment

Introduction
Mower, Reel Type
Cup Cutter
Garden Rake
Thatching Rake
Pitchfork
Aerating Tool
Cups
Pins
Tee Numerals and Markers
Cup Puller
Grass Seed
Conclusion

Introduction

I AM STARTING the body of the book with the tool list to address the price issue first. Many items: fertilizer, fungicide, herbicide, a board, hammer, hand trowel, dinner fork, and broom rake are list-less examples. Although I will explain the use of these, their cost and availability need not require their inclusion on the tools and equipment list. Their price is not an issue.

You can see the list is not very long. You already have or can acquire at garage sales or second-hand stores the majority of the list including the biggest priced item, the reel mower.

Your green will be significantly faster if you can find the mower with a wheel adjustment feature. Without it, the grass will be slightly longer and slower. Your budget may not allow buying a new mower. An old reel type will still allow you to enjoy Microgolf as I have. That is my goal.

The wheel-adjustable reel mower can then be found later. Perhaps the regular players of your course would consider chipping in, no pun intended.

You might even have memberships or a donation to play for the cup cutter or the mower that will cut shorter.

Mower, Reel Type

Five blades or more. Mowers with *both* the roller height adjustment *and* wheel height adjustment are preferred.

Necessary for the green. May be used for aprons and tees as well.

Cup Cutter

A thin wall dimension is desirable so the plug diameter is close in size to the hole left.

A plunger to discharge the plug keeps the plugs intact with least disturbance to the roots of the grass.

I initially used an artillery shell, a thin wall, but that experience taught me a lesson. I tapped the plug out by hitting the side of the shell repeatedly with a mallet because a hammer could dent the shell. The plug would not come out intact.

A professional cup cutter may be the largest priced item, but does work best.

Garden Rake

One with a flat back-edge, and stiff tines.

Back edge used for crushing dried worm castings and spreading top dressings. Tines used for sand trap maintenance during play.

Broom Rake

Broom rake used for fluffing initial height cuts of green, apron, tees, and leaf raking for remainder of the course.

Thatching Rake

The perfect rake for gathering damp worm castings. Gently drag or pull the rake toward you to remove them from the green. The cupped area of the rake collects them neatly. Empty after each rake stroke.

The rake also removes pebbles, leaves, and those darn maple leaf seeds with less stress to the green. Do not run the tines of this rake into the ground. Use it more as pulling a scoop.

Pitchfork

Use for: sculpting additional slope and undulation, lifting low areas to level during green development, and aeration.

I explained and demonstrated pitchfork lifting and pitchfork sculpting to a friend named Bob. A few days after I taught him, a neighbor of his hired a tree removal service to cut down a tree. The service truck left deep ruts in the lawn. Bob was amazed to see the driver pull a pitchfork from the truck and begin lifting the sod in the tire ruts.

Bob walked over to the tree service worker who said, "Shhh. Keep this a secret. This is the best way to re-level the lawn."

With a broad smile, Bob said, "Your secret's safe with me."

Dinner Fork

A dinner fork?! Yes, a dinner fork is for raising smaller low spots in green development, divot repair, and matching replacement plugs from previous cup holes.

I like to bend the fork's handle in half, so the end of the fork handle does not hurt my hand when I push it into the ground. Be aware of small pebbles wedging between the tines. Remove pebbles before re-penetrating the green's sod.

Aerating Tool

Three-eighths inch tool diameter maximum. Plug removal is preferred for the green. Optional, as pitchfork will work, but plug removal *is* better.

Cups

I knew a fellow who used a flower pot four inches in diameter until his cups came in the mail: he was *that* anxious to play. He found the satisfying sound of the

Tools and Equipment · 21

ball in the cup worth the effort and expense and regretted the delayed order.

Perhaps a friend at a local golf course has some used cups. A little crack in it would not be a big deal for you.

Recessing the golf cup one inch from the top level of the green maintains the integrity of the lip. Your dinner fork will help you level any roll-over of the lip. Have you extremely sandy soil? You may have the cup higher than the one inch recess to maintain the lip. When the regulation cup is installed vertically the pin will be.

Pins

You could make your own. But for durability, straightness, and aesthetic appeal, you cannot beat the real thing.

Tee Numerals and Markers

I will be numbering each tee box for order clarity and wish to eliminate unnecessary mowing obstacles.

I daydreamed about a concrete, numbered plug recessed flush into the ground. I could mow right over them. Balls would not hit them. Players would not trip over them and plugs would be difficult for someone to walk off with.

My tee markers are the shorter cuts of grass rather than objects to move every time I mow.

Cup Puller

You must have one because there is no other way to pull the cup out of its previous hole.

You can make your own by bending a J bend on the end of a quarter inch steel rod, with the J dimension smaller than the pin's hole in the bottom.

It is easier and straighter to pull the cup out when you stand erect. Hook the J through the pin's hole in the bottom of the cup. Squat down a little and pull the cup out by pushing up with your legs. This is easier and neater than pulling with

Tools and Equipment · 23

your arms as the force is straighter and your legs are stronger.

You may pull from opposite sides of the bottom cup hole alternately to start the cup out straight.

If you pull from only one direction, the cup may scour and pull up sod.

Grass Seed

My original intent was to cut my Kentucky bluegrass shorter and accept whatever grain and ball speed to take its own course. Some varieties of grass will survive your mower's lowest cut and some will not.

My philosophy now is: the variety of grass that survives the cut is the base grass, then over seed with a variety that will survive the short cut.

Bent grass seed works very well in my climate. I believe people in drier climates may want to consider Bermuda grass. Is your lawn currently green? Then you are watering enough for bent grass seed.

Conclusion

The tool list is short, the expense is nominal. A large golf course has to automate and apply chemicals to cover their territory. They have to spend money to compress time and space. The adjustable reel mower and professional cup cutter with plunger are the largest portion of the total cost. They cost far less than your time is worth. In less time than it takes to maintain your lawn or play a microgolf round and for less than a set of clubs or greens fees, you can develop your own course and play everyday.

3 Course Layout and Development

Tees
Distances
Plantings
Borders and Boundaries

Tees

FOR THE MOST TEE PLACEMENTS, keep the green central on your course layout. Placing the green centrally allows you to place tees around it in the largest number of directions. Placement of the green is the first consideration in course layout. You want to place the green with tee locations in mind.

Imagine this: if the center of the green is the center of the yard, then of the 360 degrees around the green—each tee box for nine boxes—can be every forty degrees, and eighteen tees every twenty degrees. Those directions supply tee box placements.

It is amazing how two tee boxes side by side with one yard between makes the shots to the green different, with the green's slopes, undulations, and shape you develop. This subtlety you have to experience.

Compare standing in one tee box and then the second, they are different holes from the illusion of just looking at them or seeing the box locations on a map of the course.

A tee below or above the level of the green is more challenging and a typical feature of course design. The very reason course architects design elevation changes around the greens. Take a page from their book and incorporate this practice in your tee placements.

Even on a level tee to green elevation, the plateau effect, making the apron a steeper slope than the green instills your course with the spirit of the game's beginning.

How many ways can you combine the number of tees and greens? Can you install one, two, or more greens? Is there enough room for eighteen tees or only nine? There are many combinations.

One green and nine tees is a minimal Microgolf course. Play it twice.

Two greens may be preferable if your yard has two different elevation areas. It works well to have one for each and tees in both.

You may have one large or level area. A larger green with one cup and eighteen tees or with two cups and nine tees will give you eighteen holes. Play the nine tees, first to one cup: then play a second time to the other cup. It is a free move if one cup is in your putting line to the other — not closer to the object cup. The sizes of tees or greens can affect their number.

I am limited to about one square yard — three by three feet — in most of my tee areas. This appears to be the minimum size to spread out the wear and tear on the tee box.

For consistent clean contact with the ball and distinguishability, I actually cut a shorter height grass and call that the tee box. The ball must lie within the tee box area for all tee shots, tees optional. I cut this the same height as the apron for the number of times I have to change the mower height. Remember to fluff the tees as you reduce the height and develop the apron.

Your property line may be rectangular. Fences, small gardens, ornamental trees and fruit trees, make the property line seem irregular. They can be used to make a shot's degree of difficulty. Like I find myself in by accident, such as a poorly hit approach shot that leaves me no choice but to hit over a bush and stop the ball on the green.

Design a hole over a retaining wall, embankment, or next to a stand of lilacs.

Use a ball and a sand wedge from areas that will fill the categories I've just mentioned. Experience will give you the sense of knowing where tee boxes and greens should go.

The designated tee box placement is more Microgolf than distance.

Course Layout and Development · 29

Distances

Microgolf is determined in feet, not yards, by definition. The maximum length tee shot for a green that is oval-shaped, forty feet long and twenty feet wide, is one hundred feet. The maximum length tee shot for a green twenty feet long, and ten feet wide, is fifty feet.

The distances are *actually* determined in the green and tee layouts relative to your area's size and shape.

The smallest green on my home course, the Dream Links, used for the first nine, is thirteen feet by eight feet. The longest tee shot is forty feet.

You see the distance is reduced to accommodate the green and still leave room for the tee boxes or the green size reduced to match the distance.

You measure distance for your score card from the center of the tee box to the center of the green. A large green with two cups? Use the center of each half of the green.

It may seem that a rectangle yard, the most usual, would not give distances equally. That is just what you want. Imagine tee boxes in the corners of the rectangle being maximum length holes. If you place the green slightly off-center with more space on one end of the rectangle, so much the better. A built-in stagger of distances will add to the challenge of your course.

Have you only nine tee boxes? Two pin placements make the same tee box a different hole and distance.

Distances magnify when obstacles appear in the ball's line of flight.

Plantings

The area between tee and green can be enhanced for degree of difficulty by adding landscape characteristics such as a shortly trimmed bush or yucca plant. Something that can withstand an occasional golf ball and has a full season of play. Spring flower beds that are there one season and susceptible to those occasional ball hits do not make good hazard plantings.

Plantings need not be organic. A rock garden or sand trap are two examples of 'plantings' that add to your course.

I learned a valuable lesson in the area behind my sand trap. I started with less than one mower's-width distance between a bush and the back edge of the trap. I made that area easier to maintain by making that strip one mower width so I could mow it and not have to use a trimmer.

The lesson here is to think of any of these kinds of areas either non-existent or keep these areas multiples of mower's widths rather than feet and inches, most notably, Out of Bounds.

Boundaries and Borders

Out of Bounds, or the perimeter of the course can be the neighbor's fence, an extremely high cut of grass, garden, or hedge row.

One of my out of bounds is very close, with a small landing area, so I added an extra tee box for a drop area when my ball goes O.B. there.

Be generous to a fault with areas declared to be unplayable. I put bricks or lawn edging material around unplayable areas for clarity's sake. Do not let the temptation to save a penalty stroke come at the expense of prized tulips or your clubhead. Declare it unplayable.

I prefer to allow placement of the ball rather than dropping the ball to expedite speed of play whenever required.

Whatever the distinction, be consistent for the integrity of the course. It is your course. You decide borders, boundaries and where the green is developed.

4 Green Development

Slope
Undulation
Shape
Height of Grass
Birth of the Green
Nursery
Apron
Sand Traps
Cup Cutting
Cup Placement

Slope

Slope can be either even or irregular if you lay a straightedge on the green. The profile is either a "same slope" green or a "multiple slopes" green.

It is important that the green have slope to increase challenge. There are no greens absolutely flat. Slope of the green is usually towards the direction of approach. The slope can be made or enhanced by top dressing and filling the high side higher, or by lifting sod with a pitchfork.

Lift sod by inserting the tines of a pitchfork and lifting in the direction you perceive as uphill or up slope. Lift a little at a time. Frequent lifting gradually is better than a lot at once.

You are sculpting a profile. I recommend doing this even before your grass height has achieved putting height. Slope is different than undulation.

Undulation

A roller-coaster effect to the profile of a green is more common as the difficulty of a course increases. Undulation on your green in your backyard can be as difficult or as simple as on any golf course green—even though the size of your green may be greatly restricted.

The important thing to remember is that slope changes or undulations are limited by your mower's ability to follow those contours without scalping the grass to bare dirt.

Start the contour shaping gradually and pay special attention to how your mower rides the high spots or contours as grass putting-height and shape are achieved.

Shape

Cut the shape a little bit lower than the rest of the lawn initially. That gives you an opportunity to refine the shape as you reduce the height of the grass. There may be slopes and undulations that are too abrupt or extreme, such as a dent or cavity in the ground, or areas you do not wish to include. Mow around them instead of incorporating them into the shape of the green. Shape is overlooked and under-appreciated as an important design feature.

A bump or dent may appear in the shape that will be the green. Now is the time to start sculpting the ground: making or breaking slope.

You can also fill in low spots, dressing with topsoil and sand mix. Given a choice, I would rather lift or sculpt a low spot than fill it.

No square corners. No irregularity that the mower cannot negotiate or turn within. It is tempting to match the shape of your yard and have right angle corners on the green, but resist the thought. Abrupt turns with the mower can skid the wheels, roller or both and scalp the grass.

A contoured oval, kidney-shape, and pear-shape are examples of shapes that can offer challenges by the nature of their shape and this is an opportunity to shape according to the landscape.

A kidney-shaped green next to an existing shrub, plant or small flower circle and nest the hollow of the kidney shape to that as an additional challenge. See *Front Cover*.

Green Development · 37

A bent oval around the corner of a house or shed will take advantage of L-shaped property.

Get your putter and a ball and stand in the vicinity of where you see the green, and get a feel of the shape you wish to incorporate.

The shape and placement of the green should allow 360 degree access for approach shots. Try not to put the green in the corner of the yard. Doing so eliminates using the corner as a teeing area.

The shape of the green is integral to the placement of the green and allows the most options for tee placements.

Hit the ball around your yard with a wedge and putter while imagining a par 3 hole. A chip and two putts is a par 3. Notice how the existing slope and shape of your yard can influence the degree of difficulty. There is why and where you want to start cutting.

Height of Grass

You need to consider on the course three heights of grass. A fourth is an option, and potential for a fifth grass height.

Heights of Grass

1. Green & Nursery
2. Aprons & Tees
3. Rough, the bulk of the lawn.
4. Fairway Cut, one ring around apron.
5. Heavy Rough. Beneficial next to fences and out of bounds. Helps slow errant balls and keeps ball in play and out of a neighbor's yard.

Grass height is limited by the mower. How low can the mower go?

Green speed is determined partly by the grass height but more significantly by the continuity of height and grain. The grain will develop relative to slope, sunlight or a body of water, the drainage direction.

You may be tempted to set your mower on its lowest setting and cut the shape of your green. I don't recommend it.

Always remember, never cut the grass more than half of its height at any one time. The grass needs half its length to recover from the shock of mowing. Never mow more than half, and one-third of each blade is preferred.

Birth of the Green

You will be using a rotary gas-powered mower to start with, that's what most people use on their lawns now.

Approach the first cut with caution, be certain you are cutting all the blades uniformly.

Each and every time during initial green development, fluff with a broom rake and cut the grass at the *same* height. Fluff and cut in each of *four* directions *before* you are done cutting the green. You can, for example, fluff the grass north, cut the grass, fluff the grass east, cut the grass, and so on around the points of the compass. You will see more grass needing to be cut each time you fluff. Wait three days.

Imagine that a blade of grass is laying down. The next time you fluff, you will stand that blade up and remove too much of its length and thereby kill that plant.

The technique for fluffing is neither violent nor vigorous as the grass blades will be woven together like snarled hair. Rather, drag the rake as though it were a rope.

This is how to reduce and eliminate the snarl in the grass. Fluff and cut the green gradually in this manner. Use the opportunity to alter the shape of the green as you become more familiar with it. *You* are the course architect.

Repeat at that same height, fluffing and cutting four directions as described. Fluffing and cutting twice at the same height will help cut all blades evenly before lowering the mower. Wait three days.

Green Development · 41

Lower mower height. Repeat procedure.

It may be unsettling at first to see the change from long grass to short. The number and size of bare spots will be a surprise. Do not be discouraged.

Visualize that for the best continuity and speed of the green, you want as many sprouts (plants per square inch) as possible. This density takes the longest to develop, as the grass gets shorter, the grass will send new plant stalks into the in-between areas.

The grass and overseeding with putting green seed will fill bare spots. You will be ready for the next phase when your rotary mower will go no lower, and you are confident there are no lay-down grass blades of longer length. Wait three days.

You will need two mowers. Your rotary mower for the rough and remainder of the yard, and a push reel mower to cut the green, apron, and tees.

Look at a previously cut blade of grass. The cut end will be brown. This is the scab healing the wound of the cut. When the length of the blade starts to shorten, this damaged portion is a greater percentage of the overall blade height when cut with a rotary mower.

The green height must be done with a reel mower so that the percentage of damage to the grass blade is kept to a minimum.

A reel mower from a garage sale may work just fine. In my own search, I discovered that *some* reel mowers have *two* height adjustments. These are preferred.

One height adjustment is the roller which is the active adjustment. All mowers have that.

The second height adjustment can be either multiple wheel-mounting bolt holes or a bolt in a slot so you can lower the mower housing relative to the wheels. You can raise the wheels up on the side of the mower, lowering the mower housing, which will lower the shearing blade. Lower this adjustment on the mower housing as far as possible, permanently.

Then determine the lowest practical cutting height, without scalping, of your roller adjustment. The lowest setting may cause the mower housing to scalp and kill the grass blades.

Undulations will seem to appear in your green. You have remedies or combinations: go up a notch on the roller height, smooth off the high spots by sculpting or fill in around the undulations to lessen their severity. Mark this roller height with a permanent marker, tape, or a scratch in the mower housing paint so you can have a constant to judge how much filling or sculpting is necessary.

Mower blades must be sharp. Only sharp mower blades will cut the grass blades cleanly. And the only way to sharpen a reel mower is have the sharpening done at a shop. Your rotary blade should be new or sharp as well.

The reel mower has one additional benefit. The roller helps the turf become uniform, making this mower the secret of a satisfying green.

You may use a lawn roller. I did. I was anxious to play on a smooth putting surface. I do not recommend too much rolling, be patient. It can smother the grass roots, especially when grass is damp or wet. Loose soil can stick to the roller and pull soil out of bare spots, making them lower.

It is easier to change shape and slope during the height reducing process rather than when the lowest practical setting of the reel mower has been reached. When all that has been accomplished, continue the time line.

Fluff for the last time and cut with a reel mower at the previous rotary mower height. The first cut with the reel mower is the apron. Cut the perimeter at the same height as before and the rest of the green slightly lower this first time. That will give you a parallel line to the shape of the green. That is the outside edge of the putting surface and the inside edge of the apron. This establishes your apron and green edges. For maintenance mowing cut the green first, then the apron slightly longer from then on.

Over-seed with your green's grass seed and lightly cover the seed with sand-topsoil mix about one-quarter inch. Spread the topsoil evenly. Complete the even spreading with the back side of a common garden rake—the straight edge, not the tines.

Lightly water with the mist of a spray nozzle, for example, to glue the topsoil into place, reducing wind and water erosion from a heavy rain. Wait three days.

Mist again to seal and establish seed and topsoil in place and let dry. Cut at the same height in two directions. No need to fluff or disturb the seed and soil excessively. Wait three days.

Cut a lower height with reel mower. No need to fluff. Do not remove more than half of the blade length at any one single mowing. Wait three days.

Cut at same height as last cutting. The three day waiting is an estimated time period for the grass to recover from the cutting shock. Starting the green at the peak of the grass growing season? Two days may be enough. Four days may be necessary in early spring or late fall.

Cut every three days and lower the mower every other cutting, until you reach the lowest practical height of your reel mower. Except for refinements this is your green's grass height.

Feel free to start putting on your green from the beginning. Except when new seed is taking root, there is little need to pamper the green areas while repair sod is available.

Nursery

The nursery will give you repair sod. Transplants to your green will hasten the maturing process. Start with a larger nurs-

Green Development · 47

ery. You can let some of it return to rough later.

Select a spot away from the green, tees, and high traffic areas for a nursery. Cut a place for a nursery and develop it as a green.

The soil in the area of my green was so poor that I used up the nursery and had to make a second. I wanted to cut full cup depths without running into stones and other foreign material. I dug out a trench twelve inches deep, the width of the mower and several feet long. I backfilled with sieved topsoil and clean sand mixed half and half, planted bluegrass and over-seeded with bent grass. This allowed me to cut and transfer a full depth plug for greens and aprons. See *Moving the Cup*.

Apron

The outermost edge of the green area is now your apron.

Additional slope to the apron adds challenge and better distinguishes the putting surface from the apron. It looks marvelous. The steeper slope makes the putting surface a plateau. This can be accomplished by sculpting the apron around the inside edge towards the center of the green and around the outside edge of the putting surface, towards the apron. You are effectively raising the separating edge between apron and green.

I also top dress (see *Sanding*) more heavily around the green's edge.

Greens and aprons have different slope and grass length but similar predictability during play.

Sand Traps

I recommend playing the course a number of times before deciding if a sand trap or two would add to the challenge, practice and experience of green-side bunker play.

Take a bit of string or clothesline and shape it around a likely area. Play with

Green Development · 49

the string in place to help visualize placement and shape. Have some fun with it.

Then remove the sod from the area and consider transplanting it to a bare spot in the lawn. You will need to dig deeper than the sod to ensure weed seeds will not take root. Grass and plant growth can be cultivated each time you rake the trap during play. Sprouts in sand pull out easily.

Dig approximately eighteen inches deep, sheer sides, in the shape you have laid out. Fill the bottom six inches with coarse gravel. I use broken chunks of concrete with smaller pieces of concrete filling the spaces between chunks. This will help with drainage so your trap does not turn into a water hazard.

The lowest point in the yard would not make the best place for your sand trap. Notice the drainage of the yard.

Fill the foot remaining with low clay content sand. Sand for concrete works well, but I prefer a finer sand, a smaller grain size. I buy children's play sand, prewashed. You can wash sand of excess clay. Fill a garbage can one-third full of sand and push a spray nozzle on your hose into the sand repeatedly. The clay will run out with the excess water. Remove stones from your sand by putting "hardware cloth"—a coarse metal screen—over the top of your garbage can before adding sand. You will splash stones onto the green if you leave them in the sand.

Neighborhood cats and other critters may use your sand trap as a litter-box. Use your garden rake to remove droppings before play. Clean sand will also cut down on the reuse of your sand trap that way. You may decide not to have a sand trap if this sounds as if it might be a nuisance. My sand trap is used as a litter-box less than once a week.

Twice a year, edge the sod back as it will try to encroach, or grow into the sand, to keep the edge of the trap sharp and defined.

Cup Cutting

A sharp edge on the cup hole lip depends on the cutter. I have used the cup itself, but it breaks easily. I have also used an artillery shell, but the plug of sod is difficult to remove.

A professional cup cutter is worth the investment.

The golf cup cutter is less stress on the plug. The cutter has a plunger to push the plug from the cutting head with the least amount of distortion to the plug's shape.

The first plug you cut may be discarded. Keep the plug if moving cup or transplanting. I do not advise hammering any one of the cutting tools into your subsoil. That will chip or bend the edge on stones hidden from your view. Golf courses excavate and fill with sand-topsoil mix deep enough that they will not damage the cutter. Damage to the cutter and excavating to construct greens are expensive propositions.

Push or press the cutter into the ground with your body or foot as far as you can. Remove as much of the plug as there is in the cutter, discard or transplant. Finish digging the cup hole with a hand trowel one inch deeper than the height of the cup. Carefully place the cup into the hole by hand as far as it will go. Step on the cup until flush with the ground. Do not damage the sod around the cup hole. Put a hammer handle on the inside bottom of the cup. The hammer head becomes a handle to push with. Push by squatting down until the cup bottoms out. There should be an inch of soil and grass above the top edge of the cup. Use a dinner fork to correct irregularities after inserting the cup and to repair roll-over of the lip between moves. Insert pin and play.

I leave my cups in the ground even through winter so I can play anytime the snow leaves the ground.

The sooner you install the cup and begin playing the better. Do that early in the green shortening process. The green may not be optimum, but you will get a better feeling of shape, slope, and tee and cup placements.

Cup Placement

Place your cup either: half a mower width in, or more than a mower width in from the apron. The mower wheel could damage the cup lip if the cup is exactly one mower width inside the edge. Remember the first cut on the green is that perimeter edge.

Place the cup relative to changes of slope lines or undulations. The surface characteristics are challenging aspects to your green. Find spots on your green that feel like they would be very tricky pin placements. Put the pin there on purpose. It makes Microgolf that much more fun.

Proper placement prevents problems from mower mishaps, minimizes maintenance and maximizes pleasure.

5 Time Line

Day 1
- Envision green placement.
- Envision tee placements.
- Determine shape of green.
- Fluff grass in green, apron, tee, and nursery areas. Cut shape. First cut height is a bit lower than current height. Sculpt, lift, and level wherever necessary.

Day 4
- Fluff green, tees, apron, and nursery.
- Cut green, tees, apron, and nursery same height as Day 1.

Day 7
- Fluff green and tees.
- Cut green and tees at lower height.

Day 10
- Fluff greens and tees.
- Cut greens and tees same height as Day 7.

Day 13
- Fluff greens and tees.
- Cut greens and tees at lower height.

Day 16
- Fluff greens and tees.
- Cut greens and tees same height as Day 13.
- Continue until lowest rotary mower height is achieved.

Day 19
- Fluff, for last time.
- First day to cut with reel mower.
- Distinguish green - apron height difference.
- Over-seed, top dress, lightly water.

Day 22
- Cut same height as Day 19, with distinction between green and apron.

Day 25
- Lower reel mower cutting height.

Day 28
- Cut greens, aprons, and tees same height as Day 25.

Day 31
- Cut greens, aprons, and tees at lowest reel setting for green, with apron and tees higher.
- Cut cup hole, insert cup, insert pin, and play Microgolf. Any time. If you can stand it, so can the green.

After Day 31
- Cut as often as grass doubles in height.

6 Green Maintenance

Cutting the Green
Fertilizing
Sanding or Top Dressing
Aerating
Divots
Problems

Cutting the Green

FIRST, CAREFULLY MOW THE EDGE, or perimeter of the green. Let the wheel of the mower travel a couple of inches on the apron. There is an offset between the actual cutting edge and the wheel. Sight the reel edge to the apron edge. One direction you cut may feel more natural than the other. I like to cut clockwise. The "edge cut" gives you a place to start and stop when cutting the balance of the green. Cut the remainder of the green completely in two directions perpendicular to each other.

Green Maintenance · 59

Cut the green consistently. The same cutting pattern will allow a uniform grain to develop and the roller will help to gently level the surface. The directions may be determined by undulation and slope changes. Do not let the mower straddle an undulation ridge. The mower is more likely to scalp an abrupt surface change. Sculpt out scalped undulations or changes in slope with a pitchfork for large areas and a dinner fork for small spots.

Mow across or diagonal to slope changes and undulations. Allow the mower to follow the contours. A reel mower has the ability to roller-coaster over features for the best looking green.

Fertilizing

Does your lawn look good now? Keep up the good work. The green and lawn require the same care and feeding.

Fertilizer particle size large enough to deflect a ball is a consideration for us.

Once a month I fertilize the green with liquid fertilizer on the lowest dispenser setting. I am giving the green the Tender Loving Care a golf course architect would.

Sanding or Top Dressing

Golf green architecture starts in the subsoil, fifty percent inorganic material. Fine particle size for less compaction, rapid drainage, and easy cup cutting. A softer green means the ball stops quicker.

I top dress the green once a month with very fine sand instead of the expense and work of excavating the subsoil. These are opportune times to enhance slope, the plateau effect, and undulations. Not too much at any one time: the grass is short. You do not want to bury and kill it.

By hand I broadcast the sand from a bucket. Make sure there are no stones or foreign objects large enough to interfere with the ball. Dry sand is a must so it spreads evenly. Use the back edge of the garden rake to spread the sand more evenly than any broadcasting method obtains. A walk-behind spreader leaves rows of sand that need to be leveled. The rake method of levelling the sand also works well with sand that may be blasted onto the green from the sand trap.

Bagged children's play sand works the best. Open the bag and dry the sand if necessary.

Twice a year instead of just sand—spring and later summer, for example—I will use a 50-50 mix of sand and topsoil sieved through the hardware cloth. There will still be some particles that are too large. Scoop them up with the thatching rake gently. Then lightly water with a spray—enough to 'glue' into place. Keep off until it is dry. Your feet will track up the topsoil and create low spots.

Top dressing improves slope, undulation, plateau, drainage, putting, overcompaction, and lets the roots breathe.

Aerating

Aerating is necessary. How often varies. Is your current soil soft under foot and drain rapidly? Aerate less, perhaps once a year. Soil conditions influence frequency. Foot traffic and mower roller can compact enough to smother the roots. Poor drainage encourages fungus and mold.

The best aerating method is one that removes a plug of sod. The little holes or plugs encourage air, water, nutrients, and top dressings to penetrate the turf mat more deeply. This changes the subsoil without excavating. The hole size left must be smaller than a golf ball can settle into, not larger than three-eighths inch diameter, smaller if possible. A plug removal system may not be available to you since they are normally one-half inch diameter or larger. The tines of a pitch fork repeatedly punched into the green is a reasonable alternative. I made a board with rows of nails on the face. This allows me more holes per square inch for faster subsoil penetration. Sandals with long spikes on the bottom are available at garden shops. Golf shoe spikes are not quite long enough.

I believe a four-inch penetration to be your goal. Top dress with sand and aerate a little more often than once a month if you are not getting four-inch penetration with a pitchfork to start with. You will loosen the soil quite rapidly, allow deeper penetration of the cup cutter and more complete plugs.

Moving the Cup
Also used for Damage Control
Transplanting Technique

Change of the cup to a new location is done by first following the procedure found under *Cup Cutting*. Keep the plug, then proceed as follows. The plug will not be a full diameter and height plug to fill the former cup or nursery hole.

Measure the plug height. Back fill the old hole with 50-50 topsoil-sand mix and compact with hammer handle three-quarters inch more than required. The plug on top of the backfill will stick up. One inch is too high.

The plug diameter is smaller than the hole size due to the wall thicknesses of the cutter. You need to account for this discrepancy, more compaction of the back fill and incomplete plug.

Lift the area around to the plug height with a dinner fork. Then level the plug and the area around it by compressing with the ball of your shoe or even better, by laying an oversized board on the plug area and stepping on the board.

Time to play, and remember to repair divots while you do.

Divots, and Marks on the Green

In my experience, I have yet to see the topic of green divots addressed. The paradox is that I have never seen a course,

Green Maintenance · 65

magazine, or golf show neglect to say, "Fix your divot."

How are you to accomplish that simple task, automatically, if you don't know how? I believe the act of repairing a divot has been trivialized to the point that it gets treated trivially.

I believe there are three varieties of divots. The dent, the split dent, and the dent with a dislodged portion of sod, sometimes appearing as a flap. The type and nature of the divot is determined by the soil characteristics, the density of plants per square inch, and the plants' ability to intertwine, weaving a mat.

The dent and the split dent are a function of the force of the ball. The dislodged or flap tear is from the spin of the ball.

It is common to see professional golfers on television dislodge a portion of sod when a ball contacts the green surface because they impart more backspin to the ball. The ball rotates out a piece of sod, or a flap may be glued to the back of the dent.

It is curious the divots do not appear on every green even with the same club hit the same distance and hit by the same professional golfer. This is due to varying soil and moisture conditions.

My methods and techniques can provide the opportunity to treat the subject with reflective thought. Here we go.

The Dent

The best divot tool is a dinner fork. The tines penetrate easily. The tines do not make too large a hole, and in sculpting the green the tines do not flip out easily.

Insert the dinner fork along the sides of an oval dent or at any point around a round dent. Gently lift up the low spot when the tines have reached full penetration. Lift the center of the divot higher than it was to begin with, reversing the center of the dent. A little bit several times is better than all at once.

Then re-level the surface with some flat item. This may or may not be your putter head, depending on its shape. The flat portion of your shoe is your second most available option.

The Split Dent

Proceed as before, except right after you lift the long sides of the oval—because the split dent is almost always an oval—walk the handle of the fork or divot tool towards the gash. You are trying to close the split. If you cannot, remove a little soil from the gash. That will help you draw the sides of the gash together. Lift up the tines, then walk up the handle. Lift slightly higher than the original surface, then level the spot with your shoe or putter.

Flap or Dislodged Divot

The flap or dislodged divot is slightly more difficult. First, raise the edge of existing grass, the sides of the dent, not the center. Lift and walk the fork toward the bare spot around it. Guide the flap back or insert the dislodged sod into its original position. It may require additional lifting around the flap to get the sides of the divot and the sides of the flap to meet *above* the level of original sod.

The idea is to reshape the compacted subsoil of the dent and end up with a bulge. Then flatten the area.

Use a portion of your shoe without a cleat. On many golf shoes this is the ball of the foot.

I do not like using a tee or a pencil for this procedure. Either is a single point that does not lift a portion of the sod. Both flip out, tearing the sod, and that makes a trough or furrow. They cut through rather than lift up.

You are making a trough with the main body of the divot tool or fork if you penetrate too deeply with the tines. Just the depth of the tines is deep enough.

This technique applies to gaps in the grass mat during initial development of the green. Lifting those bare spots up is preferable to rolling them out with a heavy lawn roller. You are aerating and loosening, not compacting and smothering.

An immature green is an easier pill to swallow if you get better at fixing gaps, dents, and heel marks in your line of putt during play.

Cleat Marks

Cleat marks are a different matter. They are plants ripped up out of the soil. Use a divot tool tine, a singular tine, pencil, or a tee point to push the plant back into the soil—a simple solution.

Problems & Preventions

Weeds

I prefer to mechanically remove weeds initially or as they are seen.

A medium size screwdriver with a flat blade works well. Penetrate the green at an angle toward the root of the weed with the flat of the blade up. Lift up the screwdriver blade while at the same time pulling the leaves of the weed. The screwdriver loosens the soil around the root. You can pluck the weed cleanly, root and all.

I remove a weed or two without interrupting every time I play until the full mat of grass develops.

There are many good weed-killing products on the market. I try not to overuse chemicals on the lawn. A little weed inhibitor, in the spring, is the smartest approach to chemical maintenance.

Green Maintenance · 71

Fungus & Mold

It may be difficult to distinguish whether a dying-out portion of grass is caused by fungus and mold or grubs.

Fungus and mold evidence is seen at first light of day. Their characteristic fuzz or slime withers with daylight. No foreign substances on the blades of an infected area? Then you know that it is an insect problem, *i.e.*, a critter and not a growth.

Fungus and mold become problems when moisture is high, humidity is high, temperature is high, and drainage is poor.

Sanding and aerating are allies of reducing the likelihood of fungus and mold developing. Help reduce the risk when temperature and humidity are high by not watering as often.

A nursery supply will carry and advise on the use of fungicide.

Worms and Grubs

Grubs I kill. Worms I do not. Grub preparations are available at nursery suppliers.

Worms aid in aerating more deeply than other aerating methods. They can be, however, a nuisance for the worm castings they leave every morning. But the worms are easy to harvest at night for fishing because the short grass lets you see and grab them.

You have two choices: remove the castings or break them up for top dressing. The decision depends on whether you are going to play early or delay play until the castings dry.

Remove these castings if you play early, before they get walked on. They can become a bump that will deflect a golf ball.

I remove these tiny stacks from the green and apron area by stroking the surface with my thatching rake. This soil is so rich it could act as if you have over fertilized.

A good way to top dress the green, reducing the amount of fertilizer required is leave the castings. Let dry. Add sand, pulverize and spread with back and forth motion with the back side of the garden rake.

The worms, good for your subsoil, are mostly just a nuisance on the putting surface. This little bit of maintenance, removing the castings, is also a time you can look for stray weeds or dents that did not get repaired well, or came from a larger nuisance.

Neighbors

You may not consider neighbors to be a problem at first. You will see there are issues that can arise just trying to co-exist. Keep the location of the green away from your property line to minimize the likelihood of a ball going into your neighbor's yard. You might consider a strip, a mower's width or two, of extremely high grass to act as a buffer to keep the ball in your own yard. The longest tee to green distance should also have the most margin of error, room behind the green.

Neighborhood children may decide the green to be the place to run their bicycles or skateboards, leaving elongated dents. Do not lose your temper. Repair the surface by lifting both sides of the trough with a pitchfork or fork, as if a dent, then flatten. It is amazing how fast the evidence of the trough will disappear.

It will not do any good to yell at the kids or adults who damage your green. You or someone in your family could stick a heel in the soil. It is going to happen. A gentle reminder to the kids that the green is fragile may be wise. Mention to the kids' parents to please ask the kids to refrain from playing on the green. Do not start a feud over a dent. Take heart: it is easily fixed. Areas that have been torn up beyond lifting, with the sod actually torn out, is the reason to have a *Nursery*.

Green Maintenance · 75

Transplanting is the same as *Moving the Cup*.

The neighbor invited to play is better than a tall fence to keep him out. My advice is only allow play on your course when you are present. I can see there may be exceptions to this rule. But it is best for you to have control over the course by your presence.

You may enlist a neighborhood kid to cut the green during your absence. They can appreciate the special care the green needs.

It is best to remove the pins when the course is not in play. You need not leave an open invitation to strangers or neighbors with the temptation of pins left in place. Let alone the pins' potential theft. Even if you are at home, you may not notice an intruder.

Your neighbors will be less a problem if you are considerate of them while you develop and play your course.

7 Playing by Microgolf Rules

Definition of Microgolf
Putts
Par
Order of Play
Ball Marking
Pins
Out of Bounds
Unplayable Lie
Clubs

Definition of Microgolf

O NE HUNDRED FEET MAXIMUM for any one shot. One hundred feet per leg of a dogleg hole for a par 4 or a par 5 double dogleg. Green size maximum forty by twenty feet. Eighteen holes minimum.

The leading edge of each tee box shall be no closer to the apron than the distance from apron to the center of the green along that line. A two or more cup green is defined by the center of each cup

Playing by Microgolf Rules · 77

area. The closest hole is the closest center for consideration. Implicit in this rule is that a portion of rough necessarily lie between tee box and apron.

Putts

No gimmes. All players must hole out.

Par

Par is determined as the number of strokes required to reach the green, and two putts. A fourteen foot tee shot is a stroke. Par is three, with two putts.

New players on the Dream Links argue a fourteen-foot tee shot counts as one of your putts. Then I watch them bogey my par 3. The standard practice for determining par *is* my criterion.

Some builders of Microgolf courses have a dogleg hole one shot from tee to bend of the dogleg, second stroke onto the green, and two putts. The hole is a par 4. I recommend par 3 holes are easier keeping score in your head, counting strokes or strokes over and under par. The score card is unnecessary most rounds.

Just think, you're going to have course records. High and low scores. My current course record is 13 under par and the high score record, if an honor, is 52 over par.

Order of Play

The first tee honor is the last winner. Follow in order until a lower score rearranges it. Low score goes first. First player to play their second shot is the ball farthest from the pin, until all have completed play.

A person's ball on or off the green does not determine order of play.

Lowest score plays first at the next tee. Ties in score play in previous order.

This order of play is the rule of golf. Farthest from the hole plays next.

Playing by Microgolf Rules · 79

Ball Marking

It is amazing how often one ball will be behind another, making it impossible for the ball farthest away to be played and not disturb the ball nearer.

I allow marking the ball on or off the green; mandatory marking when requested, accommodating the small area.

No player is allowed to mark their ball until everyone in the group has teed off. Inevitably, a ball on the green will be hit by a subsequent player off the tee. No penalty stroke for the hitter.

The person whose ball was hit must play his ball where it came to rest unless the hit ball goes O.B., or into an unplayable lie. No penalty stroke placing the ball back into play.

The original ball bumped into the cup? No additional stroke for the person whose ball went in the cup. That led to a discovery.

Pins

I found leaving the pins in the most practical manner of play. That's right, I leave the pin in throughout the round.

It speeds play and eliminates pin removal confusion. I said before, the order of play is the farthest from the hole regardless of the players's ball being on or off the green. No penalty stroke for hitting the pin.

This change is one of the more controversial deviations from the standard rules of golf; but over time it makes a round simpler and faster. You be the judge.

Out of Bounds

You determine the boundaries that are Out of Bounds. Use the standard rule for a ball hit O.B.: rehit from where you last hit the ball; add one stroke.

A ball hit O.B. from the tee box? Re-teeing is allowed from that tee box.

Designated O.B.s may use a specified tee box, teeing not allowed. The East property line and a portion of the South property line are so close on my course as to be unfair for the number of times the ball can be repeatedly hit O.B. I cut a nineteenth tee box for a drop area for fairness and speed of play. One stroke penalty and teeing not allowed. A local accomodation to special conditions. That means I have nineteen tee boxes.

One stroke penalty and loss of distance for Out of Bounds.

Unplayable Lie

I am generous when players want to declare a ball unplayable so they will not damage their club or portions of the property.

As I mentioned in *Borders & Boundaries*, placing rather than dropping the ball speeds up play. It is fairer for the unpredictable places the ball could bounce into and the ability to swing at the ball without tearing up shrubbery, buildings, fences, *etc.*

Placement of the ball is an abbreviation of the rules that eliminates potential confusion of how to handle a bad bounce.

Placement of the ball is not more than one club length and the reach of both arms in the direction of the most available swinging area, not closer to the pin. That means pretend your ball and pin are connected by a string. The direction of club and arm distance is along the path the ball would make swinging on that arc.

One stroke penalty, place ball not more than a club and two arm lengths, not closer to the cup.

Option Two is placing the ball at any point on the line from tee shot location and ball's landing spot not closer to the pin. One stroke penalty.

Clubs

I limit each player to a putter and one other club to keep golf gear to a minimum. Most opt for a sand wedge or pitching wedge. First time players comment having another club option or two would improve their score. Limiting the number of clubs keeps the game more fair to all participants, allows faster play, and teaches pulling shots, not clubs out of your bag.

These rule changes are argumentative and I don't expect they would be approved by the rule makers of golf; but in my experience, these changes are necessary to accommodate the small area in and around my own Dream Links.

We are the governing body for rules on our own courses.

AFTERWORD
The Dream Links Legend

M<small>Y DESIRE IN PRODUCING</small> this information is to bring Microgolf to you, dear Reader and Golfer. I have the pleasure of introducing golf to beginners, helping them realize the fun of the game. I have also offered passionate golfers a challenge and improvement of their short game prowess. A few golfers even appear intimidated by the difficulty of my Dream Links Microgolf course. Dream Links, the course, is for me the reality of a daydream and a rebuttal to the nay-sayers.

Microgolf is golf. Just think, in the space of a fat month you too will be playing on your own Microgolf course.

Tee time!

The phrase, "tee time," reminds me of the experience I had building my Dream Links Microgolf course. My first nine was done. Yet, a sense of incompleteness convinced me to consider changes.

The Dream Links Legend · 85

The number of possible tee placements virtually sprang up all over the remainder of the yard. It occurred to me, a large two cup green would take advantage of so many tees for a complete eighteen. Alas, the yard space would not accommodate increasing the green size and still have that number of tees. There—on a higher elevation—there before my eyes—there appeared the second-nine green. The tee placements, sand trap, drop tee box, all of it viewed with an inner sight, a knowing, of an existence from another time. I had already been here, seen it and played it. I was in touch with the origins of the game at perhaps the original course, for that's only what I can call it. I could see the North Sea, feel the wind and moisture on my face. The smell of wet wool and the grass after passing through the sheep. The flock's favorite grass blades shorn to the limit of their existence and the pasture's balance left idle by comparison, the leeward side of the heavy grazing bare sand from their huddle to escape the harshest blows. The herders are content with the rams, ewes, and lambs' safety and feeding. The men pause in their conversation of wool money, veterinary and a pint at the end of this glorious day, idly swing their staffs at a ball of cloth discarded nearby. One of them strikes the cloth and in a momentous flash!, the ball sails into the air, lands on the over-grazing and stops in a depression.

"I'll wager a pint ye'll nay do that to the same satisfaction."

"I'll better ye anytime to my satisfaction."

"The match is on ye son of a so and so."

So it may have been, as it is for me, and can be for you. To be at the base level of the original.

Distance defined, not distorted. Approaches experienced and repeated, not mapped and contrived. In the space of

The Dream Links Legend · 87

yards, the thrill and comfort of knowing we are the same as once we were, the spirit, camaraderie, challenge, and satisfaction sought elsewhere found on our own. The hours and acres condensed into a Microgolf course. I want you to feel the same tingle on your neck that I feel on mine when you say to your fellow 'herder', "Tee time."

Text is set in *Stempel* Garamond®, registered trademark of Linotype-Hell AG.

Text is printed on Glatfelter Authors B-05. This acid free paper is 85% recycled (10% post-consumer).

The book is bound with RepKover™ reinforced paperback-cover binding. RepKover is a trademark of Otabind International b.v.

Cover Art and Cover Design by
Brian L. McGonegal.

Book Design by David C. Enger.

Printing & Binding by Malloy Lithographing, Inc. Ann Arbor, Michigan.

Additional copies of *The Microgolf Primer* are available from:
Microgolf Press
209 Rockwell Street
Jackson, MI 49203
Remit $24.95, add your State's Sales Tax.

The authors also offer many tools through Microgolf Supply which may be reached at the same address as Microgolf Press.